Performing Arts Data Service

Creating Digital Audio Resources:
A Guide to Good Practice

Nick Fells
Pauline Donachy
and Catherine Owen

edited by
Catherine Owen and Kate Iles

Produced by Oxbow Books on behalf of the Arts and Humanities Data Service

ISBN 1 84217 038 4
ISSN 1463 - 5186

A CIP record of this book is available from the British library

This book is available direct from

Oxbow Books, Park End Place, Oxford OX1 1HN
(Phone: 01865-241249; Fax: 01865-794449)

and

The David Brown Book Company
PO Box 511, Oakville, CT 06779, USA
(Phone: 860-945-9329; Fax: 860-945-9468)

or from our website
www.oxbowbooks.com

Printed in Great Britain by
The Information Press, Eynsham, Oxford

Contents

Acknowledgements

We would like to thank the following people for their contributions and support in producing this guide.

Carola Böhm, University of Glasgow

Kate Iles, Performing Arts Data Service

Edward McGuire

Damian Robinson, Archaeology Data Service

MusicWeb Consortium

1. Overview of the guide

This guide is intended as a basic 'how to' for those wishing to use audio materials in the creation of digital resources. It deals with such issues as copyright, choosing equipment, playing audio media, delivery of audio to users, data management and preservation. It is not intended to be an exhaustive guide. It will almost certainly be necessary for you as the resource creator to consult additional more specialised sources according to your particular needs.

The most important first task for anyone considering audio digitisation is to assess the scale of the project. This guide should help, and although the sections may be read and used as self-contained units, it is advisable initially to read the guide as a whole and acquire an understanding of the main issues. This could save you time and money later.

What follows is a brief summary of each chapter.

2. Working with copyright

   An overview of UK copyright law and the way it affects digital resource creation. In particular, issues surrounding the copying and distribution of audio materials, including musical materials, are discussed. A practical approach to applying for and negotiating copyright licences is outlined.

3. Digitising audio: an outline

   A broad outline of digitisation, highlighting its advantages and potential pitfalls. A general description of the resources required is followed by a technical appendix explaining digital audio in more detail.

4. Some note on playing back analogue audio media

   This chapter considers some commonly used analogue audio media on which your source materials may reside, such as analogue tapes and LP records.

5. Computers for audio

   An outline of the various common computer platforms which might be used to digitise audio, with a discussion of the strengths and weaknesses of each. Guidance is given about how to make informed choices about audio hardware.

6. Other resources: skills and time

   A brief outline of the technical skills required of digitisation, along with a discussion of the factors which will affect the time required to complete the project.

7. Creating the digital audio files: a step-by-step guide

   The basic steps involved in transferring sound recordings from analogue and digital media to computer, and an outline of various post-digitisation tasks which may need to be carried out.

8. Managing and documenting the data

    An introduction to cataloguing resources, explaining associated concepts such as metadata and standards. The reasons for creating metadata for digital resources are discussed and advice offered on how to go about creating a useful metadata record.

9. Presentation and delivery

    Information on some of the ways sound can be presented to users, considering downloading sound from the web, audio streaming, data compression, and presenting sound from CD-ROM. This also considers design aspects of incorporating audio into the resource, as well as access issues.

10. Preservation

    This considers the development of a strategy for preserving your digitised audio, both in terms of backing up the data and of maintaining support for file formats in the long term.

2. Working with copyright

2.1. INTRODUCTION

Although this may not seem the obvious topic for the first chapter of a Guide to digitising audio, intellectual property rights in your resource are the first consideration when planning a digitation project. Gaining permission for use of audio resources can be time consuming and costly, and should be scheduled early in the planning stages of a project. This chapter presents a general introduction to some of the practical implications of copyright in relation to digitising audio. The sections below give advice on current UK legislation, how to identify copyright in a work, and how to obtain copyright permissions and clearances for the sound that you digitise.

It should be emphasised that there are no international copyright laws. Each country has an individual approach to intellectual property. There are, however, international conventions and treaties – the Universal Copyright Convention (UCC) and the Berne convention – that promote reciprocity between countries and a general standard of protection. This does not mean, however, that the law in every county is the same, and in some the level of protection and support for maintaining copyright is so low that they are excluded from such treaties. This chapter aims therefore to outline copyright laws mainly with reference to the UK *Copyright, Designs and Patents Act 1988*. If in doubt about any copyright matters it is always recommended that you seek help from an Intellectual Property or Copyright lawyer.

2.2. COPYRIGHT IN PRACTICE

When digitising audio you may be:

- making original recordings
- using existing recordings
- storing or archiving recordings in a database
- using recordings to create CDs, web sites and/or making them available to the public (i.e. to more than just yourself)
- using audio for private research or study

In the above cases, except for private research or study (see section 2.3.5 on 'Fair Dealing'), it will probably be necessary for you to gain the permission of the owner of copyright(s) in the work before you can use the audio material.

'Why bother?' is often a common question asked in relation to copyright. Apart from the fact that using someone else's material without their permission is illegal, there are ethical reasons why it should be adhered to:

- Intellectual property often takes significant time and effort to create and creators should, at the very least, be asked permission for its use.
- Audio resources are often valuable commodities and the entertainment industries are particularly vulnerable to IPR abuses. They are quick to litigate.
- Using material without asking permission or giving acknowledgement and recompense means that there is less incentive for the owners to continue to create, and use of the work becomes more expensive.

This last point is very significant. It is like a chain reaction. If no recompense is given to the creators, there is less incentive to be creative; therefore less work will be produced, and the work will be more expensive. This means there is less incentive to obtain the rights, and in turn less income and incentive for the creators, and so on. In order to stop this chain reaction, to keep prices for obtaining copyright low, and to encourage authors to create, the 'right to copy' needs to be obtained.

2.3. SUMMARY OF THE LAW

The UK *Copyright, Designs and Patents Act 1988* aims to encourage the creation of works by giving support and protection for individual effort; negatively, it exists to prevent others from using the efforts of creators for their benefit without proper recompense or acknowledgement.

2.3.1. What is copyright?

Copyright is an Intellectual Property (IP) right given to the creators of works that are:

- original

and

- recorded in writing or otherwise.

Copyright protects nine different categories of work: literary, dramatic, artistic, musical, sound recordings, films, broadcasts, cable programmes and typographical arrangements of published editions. As long as a work is stored electronically or otherwise, or is expressed in some sort of physical or fixed format (there is no copyright in an idea), and as long as some original effort has gone into it, then the work automatically holds copyright in the UK.

In some countries (the US for example) it is necessary to register your work with a copyright body; this is not the case in the UK. In America it is also necessary to put the copyright symbol (©), your name and the date on your works to have them acknowledged and under copyright. Using the copyright symbol, name and date is also a requirement of the UCC treaty, and although it is not a requirement in the UK, it is a good idea to use this convention for new works.

For recorded works it is usual to encounter a number of individuals or institutions who each have rights in the work. A commercial recording of a contemporary piece for chamber ensemble may, for example, attract multiple rights associated with the composer of the work, the publisher of the work, each individual musician and the record company or persons responsible for the mechanical recording of the work.

2.3.2. Who owns it?

Intellectual property, as with all other types of property, has an owner or multiple owners. The copyright owner is normally the author/creator of the work. If the work has two or more owners, then each have separate and independent ownership in the copyright work. In some cases (when a work is created in the course of employment, for example) the copyright is held by the employer rather than the creator, although freelancers do hold copyright in their work. In other cases (sound recordings, films or computer-generated works for example) the owner is the 'person by whom the arrangements necessary for the making of the recording are undertaken'.

As with ownership of other types of property, the copyright owner can transfer or assign ownership to another party: it can be inherited, or sold to a publisher for example. The copyright owner can license the use of all, or parts, of their rights in the work for any duration wished. This is the basis for most copyright contracts: monetary recompense for use of the copyright material. With advances in technology and the prominence of IP rights on the Internet, it is generally best not to grant unlimited licenses or assignments.

2.3.3. How long does it last?

The duration of copyright differs depending on the type of work that the intellectual property relates to. Copyright exists for:

- 70 years in literary, artistic, dramatic and musical works.
- 50 years in computer generated works, sound recordings and films.
- 25 years in typographical arrangements.

This duration starts from either:

- the end of the calendar year of the death of the author (or the last of the authors if it is a jointly authored work)

or

- the end of the calendar year that the work was first made available to or first shown to the public: for example the year when the edition was published, the broadcast was made, or the film screened, whichever is later.

So, if an author dies on the first of January 1929, the remaining 70 years of copyright will start from the first of January 1930 (i.e. after the end of 1929): copyright will expire on the first of January 2000 and the work will then be in the 'public domain'.

2.3.4. What is 'infringement'?

It is an infringement of copyright to do the following in relation to a work under copyright, whether in whole, part, directly or indirectly:

- copy (i.e. reproduce in any material form, including storing by electrical means)
- issue copies to the public
- perform in public
- show in public
- play in public
- broadcast
- include in a cable programme
- make an adaptation (recorded in writing or otherwise)
- any of the above in relation to an adaptation
- allow others to do these things by granting them a licence/authorising/providing the material for them to do so
- earn money from any of the above without the permission of the copyright holder

Infringements of copyright are civil, and sometimes criminal, offences. They are normally settled in a Court of Law, and repercussions for infringing copyright are normally monetary recompense, cessation of the infringing act, and reclaiming or destroying offending items. Some infringements do incur prison sentences, especially concerning piracy of CDs and computer programmes. As the prominence of IP rights, and copyright in particular, are being pushed into the foreground by advances in technology, there is a parallel increase in court cases and settlements for infringement.

2.3.5. What about 'Fair Dealing'?

There are caveats allowing limited use of copyright works for specific purposes. One of the most well-known of these is 'Fair Dealing'. Fair dealing allows the use of short extracts from a work, as long as they are not the 'essence' of the work and as long as they are accompanied by 'sufficient' acknowledgement. They may be used for:

- research or private study of artistic, literary, dramatic, musical works and typographical arrangements
- criticism or review
- reporting current events (but this does not apply to photographs)
- instruction or preparation for instruction, or for purposes of an exam so long as it is:
  - done by the person giving or receiving instruction, and
  - not done by means of reprographic process – especially concerning use of music by an examination candidate performing the work.

2.3.6. What about 'Moral Rights'?

The copyright owners have other rights which should be taken into account. The most important of these is their Moral Right to:

- paternity
  The right to be identified as the author, director, or performer of the work
- integrity
  The right to object to derogatory treatment of the work. 'Derogatory treatment' means any addition to, deletion from, alteration to, or adaptation of the work which causes distortion, mutilation or anything 'prejudicial to the honour or reputation of the author or director'
- false attribution
  The right to object to a 'statement express or implied as to who is the author / director', made by anyone involved 'knowing or having reason to believe that the attribution is false'
- privacy of certain photographs and films

Moral rights can be waived or given up by the copyright owner if desired – conditionally or unconditionally for any specified length of time. But, unlike copyright, it is not possible for an individual to assign their moral rights to another individual.

This is by no means a comprehensive guide to the law, and it is recommended that for more information on exactly what the law says you should consult the UK *Copyright, Designs and Patents Act 1988*. There are also various web sites summarising the law, and there is an online version of the UK Act (and those of numerous other countries) available in the *Collection of Laws for Electronic Access* provided by the World Intellectual Property Organisation (WIPO): http://clea.wipo.int.

2.4. MAKING ORIGINAL RECORDINGS

This section deals with situations where you need to make recordings yourself, rather than using those which already exist.

Initially, you need to identify whether the works you wish to use are protected by copyright. If so, you need to know for how long, and who owns the copyright (see section 2.3 'Summary of the Law' above).

Not only does the work (the speech, song…) have copyright, but the person performing the work (the orator, orchestral player…) also has the right to be asked permission to be recorded. You need to get permission (preferably in writing) from the copyright owner, and the performers (who have copyright in the performance), before recording the work. There is no copyright in 'natural sounds' (birdsong, traffic noise…) except for the rights of the person making the recording – which in this case will be you!

Once recorded with permission, you have the copyright in that particular recording of the work, just as a record company has the copyright in a specific CD recording.

If you intend to make the recording available to the public (if it is to be put onto a web site, for example) then this should be clearly indicated when asking for permission to record (see section 2.7 'Applying for Copyright') as the recording will then become available to a number of users; the copyright owner needs to be aware of this.

If you intend to digitally archive or store the work in a database, you must also have the permission of the performers and copyright owners by law, and if you have put organisation and creative effort into the database collection, then that is protected too. (See the UK Data

Protection Act 1988 – http://www.hmso.gov.uk/acts/acts1998/19980029.htm, and the UK Database Act – http://www.hmso.gov.uk/si/si1997/1973032.htm). You should ask permission for this at the same time as requesting permission to record and obtaining copyright clearances.

2.5. USING EXISTING RECORDINGS

This section deals with situations where you are using material from recordings which already exist.

In such situations there is also copyright in the recording itself: this is in addition to the performing and authorship copyrights. Therefore you need to identify the copyright holder of the particular recording you are using from the sleeve notes, inlay booklet, or other documentation of the recording, and ask their permission for using that recording. The copyright holder is normally identified by marks such as '© Sony Music Publishing 1990' or by words such as 'all tracks published by EMI Music Publishers'.

You should also take a note of the following details for your own reference and in case you do have trouble identifying the author or re-locating the recording:

- Title of the recording and number of the track
- Album or work it is taken from
- Composer/Author and Performer
- Arranger and Conductor if it is a musical work
- Publisher
- Date it was published
- Serial number of the recording, to aid in identification

If the recording comes from the Internet then copyright law protects it equally. There is normally a copyright notice or a contact email address on most web sites, and when locating the copyright owner of the source it is normally to that address that you should apply for help in the first instance.

It is important, especially with musical works, to identify the owners of all the various rights present in a work. Not only is there copyright existing in the work itself, but also in the specific recording used and the performance itself (i.e. the performers have rights). Furthermore, if you wish to use a printed version of lyrics, for example, then you will also need to obtain permission from the copyright owners of the typographical arrangement (the visual image of the page), and if you wish to synchronise the music with a video clip, then you will need permission to do that. It is necessary to identify and obtain all the rights in a work before using it, especially if you are presenting the work to the public (via a web site, for example).

Again, if you want to digitally store and archive your audio recordings, then you must ask the permission of the copyright owners at the same time as requesting copyright permissions and clearances. (For more information, look at the UK Data Protection Act 1988 – http://www.hmso.gov.uk/acts/acts1998/19980029.htm, and the UK Database Act – http://www.hmso.gov.uk/si/si1997/1973032.htm).

2.6. IF YOU CANNOT IDENTIFY WHO OWNS COPYRIGHT...

There is, unfortunately, no single place or organisation in the UK that holds a list of copyrights and copyright owners (as it is necessary to register copyright in the US and other countries, it can be easier to trace copyright owners there). Also, the fact that copyright is a property right can complicate matters further insofar as ownership of the property can be transferred to other parties (such as individuals or businesses) through inheritance, licensing, acquisitions or mergers.

If you cannot identify who owns the copyright for the work or recording that you wish to digitise, then there are organisations that do have listings for specific types of works (musical, literary, photographic etc); if they cannot help they should be able to direct you to a more appropriate body who can. You need to get as many details of your source material as possible, and then either approach one of the following organisations, or look on the Internet, or in catalogues/directories, or do all of these. Alternatively, you could use a copyright clearance centre that may charge you for this service.

In the UK, for example, you could approach:

- Music organisations:
  MCPS – Mechanical Copyright Protection Society – for any audio recordings
  PRS – Performing Rights Society – for broadcasts and performances of the music
  MPA – Music Publishers' Association – other inquiries
- Other Musical and Audio sources:
  National Sound Archive
  Individual Record Companies
  MCPS (on behalf of the record companies)
- Literature and Written bodies:
  CLA – Copyright Licensing Authority
  PA – Publishers' Association
  ALCS – Authors' Licensing and Collecting Society
  The Composers' and Artists' Yearbook
- Photographs and Visual Images:
  Libraries
  Artists Listings

If you are unable to identify the copyright owner for a work by 'reasonable inquiry' you may still be able to use the work by proving that you have used your best efforts and gone to a reasonable length to discover who the copyright owner is. Be very wary of this, as it is not a failsafe option: it can be very difficult to prove successfully that 'best effort' was made, and you can still be charged with infringing the copyright in a work (regardless of any caveat) if you have used it without permission.

One of the best ways to prove that you have done your utmost to identify the copyright owner is to keep a record (preferably written) of all your correspondences and contact with copyright holders. This is also one of the best ways to protect yourself from being accused of copyright infringement: by ensuring that any permissions or licenses that you may get are in writing, signed and dated. If you are in any doubt, get the agreement checked out with a copyright or IP lawyer. Keep these records for as long as you need to use the work.

2.7. APPLYING FOR COPYRIGHT

Once you have identified the copyright owner, the next step is to contact them indicating the:

- Title of the extract/recording/image that you wish to use
- Author/composer/arranger
- Date of publication
- Source where you found the work – i.e. web site/journal/CD etc.
- Length of the extract – in minutes/bars etc.
- How precisely it is to be used – i.e. for academic/educational/non-profit-making/ commercial purposes
- Media to be used – i.e. CD/CD-ROM/web site/printed copy
- Who the audience is going to be – i.e. limited access to project members/by password on the web
- Length of time it is to be used for – i.e. unlimited/estimated length of project/one month/ one year...

Stress, when contacting the copyright owner, if the use is non-profit-making, non-commercial, educational, password controlled, limited in access and any other limitations. If the copyright owner is aware that is it not being used as a money-making scheme, and that it will not be made available to everyone and anyone around the globe, then you are more likely to get a favourable response. You could also consider asking whether there are any licensing schemes that your project could take advantage of. These might include standard contracts specifying length, amount or duration limitations for education, non-commercial or other common or standard requests.

Remember also that copyright owners do have the right to be acknowledged and recompensed for use of their work, so there is normally a fee requested and may be conditions attached to your use of their work. You have to assess how the work is going to be used at present and in the future, and then decide whether you are willing to accept possible restrictions on usage and time in order to get access to the work, or whether you are willing to pay the price for unlimited access.

Give the details as specifically as possible, but do be aware that any such correspondence becomes the basis of your request. This can become an official agreement very quickly, so think about what you want and the areas that you are willing to compromise on before you contact them: and remember to keep copies of all contact with copyright owners.

2.8. WHAT NEXT?

Don't expect an immediate answer from the copyright owner, as often it will not be forthcoming. Requests normally need to be looked at by a legal expert and someone who can take a decision as to what rights you can use and for how long. If your application has been rejected, you cannot use the work. Not only would it be effectively stealing their work, but they are also now aware of your intention to use the work, and will be looking out for it. Furthermore, the courts take a very stern view of using a work after permission has been expressly denied, and the repercussions may be even more severe.

There are all sorts of reasons why copyright may be refused. The copyright owner may already have a similar project in hand that your proposal may harm, the owner may be restricted by other agreements, or the owner may simply not like your intended use of their work. Give yourself plenty of time to get a response, and have a backup plan in mind.

You should also be aware of the reasons why it may be difficult (or expensive) to get permission to use some works on the Internet. Some copyright owners are particularly wary of allowing use of their work on the Internet as it is not felt to be a medium through which their 'copy rights' are upheld, in addition to the fact that technology is developing so rapidly. If a work is used in a web site it can then be accessed by a wide variety of people in a vast array of countries. Not only this, but the work can also be copied, altered and stored by various means. Digital copying and alteration is much quicker, easier and produces much better results than other means – photocopying, for example – and as such, it is only natural that copyright owners feel their rights (both Moral and Intellectual Property rights) to be in danger. In addition, although copyright law applies to the Internet as much as to any other medium or resource, in the past it has been more difficult to enforce. This is now rapidly changing with encoding, watermarks, and other technological advances.

If you are granted copyright follow the agreement precisely: this is now a formally binding contract, and if you do not abide by the agreement then the copyright owner is within their rights to sue you.

2.9. AND FINALLY…

Some points to bear in mind:

- Plan ahead
  When considering the audio materials you wish to use for a project think about copyright as far in advance as you can – during the decision-making and selection process if possible. This cannot be stressed enough, as obtaining copyright for works can be time consuming and costly, and can ruin the aims of a project if left to the last minute. Try to plan-in copyright acknowledgements and notices in advance – especially when they are to appear in a web site for example, and try to ensure that they are prominently placed. This will normally be a pre-requisite of any copyright permission you will get. Also, remember to include possible costs for copyright clearances in the budget for the project.

- Use out-of-copyright works
  To try and avoid copyright implications entirely, it is best to use works that are:
  - More than 70 years old for literary, artistic, dramatic and musical works.
  - More than 50 years old for computer generated works, sound recordings and films.
  - More than 25 years old for typographical arrangements.
  If you are in any doubt about the status of a work, check it out with a proper authority, such as those mentioned in section 2.6 above.

- Have a backup plan
  It is always a good idea to try and be as flexible as possible with your materials, and do have a backup plan just in case you cannot obtain the copyright you want.

- Keep a record of your attempts
  Not only for your own reference, but also in case you decide to risk having to prove that your 'best efforts' were made to obtain copyright (see section 2.6 above).

- Don't forget rights exist on the Internet
  It is important to note that copyright pertains to the Internet as much as is pertains to any other media: as long as the work is original and in some sort of fixed format. Copyright extends to works in 'machine readable' format such as those stored by electronic means and electronic retrieval systems: i.e. literature, images and sound recordings on the web. Many people think of the web as a free resource pool, wherein they can copy, save and download at will. Unfortunately, this is not the case. Copyright law applies equally to sources on the web as it does to physical material in books or audio recordings, and although it has been more difficult to enforce, technology is fast developing and watermarks and security – especially pertaining to music – are big issues. In addition to this, as previously stated: if someone has put the work in and created something good enough to use then it should be recognised as such, and they have the right to be asked and recompensed for its use. Treat web resources exactly as you would audio and visual resources elsewhere.

- Remember your work also has copyright
  Not only should you be aware of the copyright in other people's material, but you should also remember that all of the above applies to your audio recordings, web sites and databases too. It is always a good idea to have some sort of copyright statement attached to your recordings and web sites indicating that you hold the copyright in it. You should make it clear that the sources you have used (especially on web sites) have been used with permission of the copyright holders, and are not to be copied or used for other purposes without the consent of the copyright owner.

- Variation from country to country
  Please bear in mind that this general introduction to copyright and copyright procedures is based on the UK *Copyright, Designs and Patents Act 1988*, and may differ from the copyright law of the country you are in. There are international treaties that encourage reciprocity of copyright terms and conditions (such as the Berne convention and the UCC convention) but there are no international laws. If in any doubt, you are advised to contact an Intellectual Property or Copyright lawyer for clarification.

3. Digitising audio: an outline

3.1. WHAT IS DIGITISATION?

Digitisation is converting something into digital or numerical form. Usually this means taking something which exists in a physical medium and making a digital copy or representation of it; this digital copy can then be stored, manipulated and distributed electronically, without the need for any physical medium.

A photograph, for instance, is an image on paper. By digitising, we convert the image into numbers which can be stored on computer. The collection of numbers represents the image: it is a copy. We no longer need to deal with the photographic paper in order to view the image.

Similarly, we can digitise sound recordings which might be on magnetic tape, for example. By digitising, we convert the sound into numbers which can be stored on computer. The collection of numbers represents the sound: it is a copy. We no longer need to deal with magnetic tape in order to listen to the sound.

3.2. WHY DIGITISE SOUND RECORDINGS?

Digital copies of recordings have some important advantages over analogue ones.

- Digital copies are infinitely repeatable: once in the digital domain, further copies can be made without loss of quality. Analogue tape-to-tape copies, for instance, degrade with each generation.

- Digital copies are easily stored: a computer can store huge quantities of digital sound obviating the need for bulky archives of tapes or disks.

- Digital copies do not degrade in a way which affects sound quality: when analogue media degrade, sound quality is lost, such as when records become scratched. Constant sound quality is maintained throughout the life of a digital copy.

- Digital data may be searched easily: a computer can be used to perform complex searches on large collections of sounds very quickly.

3.3. WHAT ARE THE PITFALLS?

- 'Digital' is not synonymous with 'high quality': this is sometimes falsely implied. Digital audio can be of lower quality than analogue audio. In some cases, digitisation of a recording can reduce sound quality. A good digital copy is one which captures as much information from the original as possible, even if the original is badly degraded. There are ways to improve the perceived sound quality of a recording once digitised. This will be discussed in section 7.5.

- Copyright is easily infringed: once digitised, the ease of making further copies and distributing them (particularly via the Internet) means it is very easy to infringe copyright. This is currently a major source of concern within the commercial music industry. It is vital to ensure you are working within the law. This topic has been covered in chapter 2.

- Digital copies still rely on some storage medium (such as computer hard disk or compact disk), which are themselves subject to physical degradation. Though degradation of digital media does not result in progressive loss of sound quality, it may eventually render data unusable. This need never be a problem, as electronic data are easily preserved by making backup copies. This is covered in chapter 10.

3.4. WHAT RESOURCES ARE NEEDED TO DIGITISE AUDIO?

- Equipment: the equipment you will need depends on the medium of your original recordings. In general, you will need a machine to play back the recordings and a machine to make the digital copies (usually a computer). In some cases this will be all the equipment you need, in others the requirement will be more complex; some tasks may need highly specialised equipment, and possibly dedicated space such as a recording studio. Equipment is discussed more fully in chapters 4, 5 and 7.

- Time: you will need to allow plenty of time for digitisation. Precisely how much will vary with each individual case: for example, some projects may involve preparation of specialised equipment, whereas others may use a straightforward technical setup. The time requirement is discussed in section 6.2.

- Skills: you may have the necessary expertise to carry out your digitisation project, or you may need assistance from other individuals or agencies. This obviously has funding and time implications which will need to be thoroughly considered beforehand. This is discussed in section 6.1.

3.5. TECHNICAL APPENDIX: DIGITAL AUDIO

This section describes digitisation in more technical detail. It may be skipped if all you need is a basic overview.

3.5.1. Analogue and digital sound

When a sound is first recorded onto a physical medium such as magnetic tape, it is converted initially into an electrical signal by a microphone. This electrical signal can in turn be converted into magnetism, which is used to magnetise a metal coating on the tape. This is an *analogue* process; the magnetism fluctuates continuously in sympathy with the fluctuations in air pressure which constitute the original sound. The tape contains a magnetic imprint, an analogous copy, of the sound. `

On playback, the magnetic fluctuations caused by the tape movement are converted back to electrical signals, and then ultimately back into sound by a loudspeaker.

A record player works in a similar way, except that here the electrical fluctuations are used to cut a groove in a disk: on playback, the groove creates a physical movement of the stylus, which is converted back into electrical signals and so on.

In the case of early gramophone and phonograph recording, the sound pressure waves were converted directly into physical movement in order to make an imprint on the medium. No electrical signals were involved at all.

Digital audio works differently. It still requires the air pressure to be converted into an electrical signal, so it relies on some of the same technology (microphones and loudspeakers in particular). But what happens to the signal subsequently is different.

In digital audio, very rapid measurements are made of the strength of the electrical signal. Each measurement corresponds to the loudness of the sound at that instant. These measurements are made by a device called an *analogue to digital converter*, abbreviated to *ADC*, which produces a numerical value for each measurement. This process is called *sampling* and the measurements are called *samples*. In most digital audio situations, samples are taken many thousands of times per second and the numbers are stored in electronic 'memory' chips, either inside a computer or in some dedicated device such as a digital recorder. Ultimately the data may be stored on the computer's hard disk, or onto magnetic tape: in this case the tape records magnetically encoded numerical data, not a direct magnetic imprint of the sound as an analogue tape recorder would.

To playback the sound, the process is done in reverse. A *digital to analogue converter*, or *DAC*, is used to convert the samples back into a fluctuating electrical signal which can then be converted into air pressure waves by a loudspeaker.

3.5.2. Resolution and sound quality

The division of the sound into discrete samples means that there is some loss of information. The process fails to capture fluctuations in the signal which happen in the time interval between one sample and the next. Similarly it fails to capture fluctuations which are smaller than its measurement steps. So the resolution of the sampling process determines how much information about the sound is captured and how much is lost.

Fortunately our hearing has limited resolution. If sufficient information is present in the sound, we don't perceive any losses; they are there, they're just below the threshold at which our aural system is able to discriminate. So if we use a high enough resolution, we can capture enough sonic information to make it seem that all the sound is there.

The sampling resolution is determined by how finely the process measures time, and how finely it measures signal magnitude. The first aspect is called the *sampling rate*, and it corresponds to the number of samples taken per second. It is measured in *Hertz*, the unit of frequency (abbreviated to *Hz*). One Hertz corresponds to one sample per second, and one *kilohertz (kHz)* corresponds to one thousand samples per second.

The second aspect is variously called *sample resolution*, *sample width*, or *bit width*. It relates to the number of dynamic levels which the process can measure. A sampling process with low resolution might be able to measure 4 different dynamic levels, from the softest to the loudest. This would be a very limited sampling process. One with a high resolution might be able to measure 100,000 levels or more. The sample resolution is determined by the number of binary digits (or *bits*) used to measure and store the data. If more bits are used, more dynamic levels can be measured and stored. If 2 bits are used, this gives 4 levels. If 3 bits are used, this gives 8 levels. If 16 bits are used, this gives 65536 levels.

The minimum resolution for basic, full-bandwidth reproduction of sound (i.e. where for many purposes the losses can be considered imperceptible) would use a sampling rate of 44.1 kHz and 16-bit sample width. Current professional recording practice generally uses systems with higher resolutions.

In addition, digital recording systems use 'error correction', whereby loss of information due to degradation or corruption of the 'carrier' of the digital data is compensated for. This results in a smooth audio signal even when there are some errors in reading the data from the medium, and thus maintains audio quality. However, it also means the listener is generally unaware when the medium is about to become unplayable, and this must be kept in mind when dealing with digital audio media for preservation purposes (see chapter 10).

4. Some notes on playing back analogue audio media

The recordings you want to digitise may reside on just one type of analogue medium, or may use several different media. If all the sound is on one medium, this makes the digitisation task much easier as only one type of playback machine is needed.

Some analogue recording media are easier to deal with than others. Old and obsolete media such as phonograph cylinders or gramophone disks will require appropriate historical equipment for playback, and the media themselves may be extremely delicate. They will need to be acoustically recorded, and this would normally need to be done in a recording studio. Other media, such as LP records and cassette tapes, use readily available playback equipment which can be connected to the computer for digitisation.

This chapter gives some brief information on the more common analogue audio media. It does not give information on how to connect and set up playback equipment.

4.1. LP AND EP RECORDS

Vinyl LPs have been one of the most popular formats for music reproduction, but they are very susceptible to dust accumulation, scratching and warping.

It is important to use a good quality turntable for digitisation, and also to place it so that it is isolated from contact with any source of mechanical vibration. Record styli and cartridges tend to act like contact microphones – a turntable stood on a table which itself is on a wooden floor, for example, will tend to pick up footsteps, doors banging and so on.

4.2. OPEN REEL TAPE

Open reel tape consists of magnetic-coated tape wound onto a plastic or metal spool or reel. There are several formats, defined in terms of the physical width of the tape in inches, including ¼-inch, ½, 1, and 2-inch. The narrower formats are usually used for recording in mono or stereo; in stereo recording, the recording machine would record on two bands or 'tracks' along the length of the tape, one track taking sound for the left hand speaker and one for the right. The wider formats are used for multitrack recording, where the tape is divided into 4, 8, or 16 or more tracks, allowing many sounds to be recorded onto the same tape simultaneously whilst the volume of each remains independently controllable.

Open reel tape machines are available from professional audio suppliers. They have electronic signal outputs, so they can be connected directly to other audio equipment and computers.

Whilst stereo connection to a computer is fairly simple, these machines do have a complex technical setup procedure requiring specialist skills. If the tape is in a multitrack format, either each track needs to be digitised separately (which would require multi-channel audio hardware for the computer), or a *mix* needs to be made which would require the use of a suitable mixing console and would be best undertaken in a recording studio.

4.2.1. Noise reduction

With any analogue audio tape, there is always background hiss evident on playback. Various methods have been used to overcome this, involving electronic circuitry to process the sound as it is recorded onto the tape (a process called *encoding*), and then again as it is played back (called *decoding*). If noise reduction was used in recording the sound, it must be used to play it back. Also, it is crucial to use the same kind of noise reduction. If an encoded tape is played back without appropriate decoding, then the hiss may be much louder than if no noise reduction had been used at all, and the sound may be distorted in other ways too.

The most widely used types of noise reduction are those developed and marketed by Dolby Laboratories (*Dolby A* and *Dolby SR* are their proprietary NR methods for professional use, whilst *Dolby B, C* and *S* are those designed for domestic cassette machines). Another fairly common noise reduction system is *dbx*.

Open reel tape machines usually require separate noise reduction units to be connected: they are not built into the machines. Noise reduction units are also available from professional audio suppliers.

4.3. CASSETTE TAPES

Cassettes operate on the same principle as open reel magnetic tape. There is only one format, designed for domestic rather than professional audio use: the tape is divided into four tracks, only two of which are played back at a time (comprising left and right; the other two play back when the cassette is turned over). There is one major drawback with cassette: the narrowness of the tape generally results in lower quality sound reproduction than with wider tape formats. For this reason it has never been regarded as a suitable medium for professional audio work.

Though cassette is now less popular than it used to be, cassette machines are still mainstream domestic hi-fi equipment. Professional machines are also available. For digitisation purposes, it is best to use a machine that will get the maximum quality of reproduction from this limited medium. There are some good cassette machines on the domestic hi-fi market at relatively low cost, and it may be worth investigating these before spending money on professional level equipment.

4.3.1. Noise reduction

Noise reduction is used on cassette tape for the same reason as open reel tape. The commonest types are Dolby B, Dolby C, and Dolby S. Most cassette machines have one or more of these built in, with a switch on the front panel. As with open reel tape, it is important to use the same kind of NR to decode a tape as was used to encode it.

5. Computers for audio

As well as considering the equipment required to play back your source recordings, you need to consider the equipment to convert your analogue sources into digital audio files on computer. In general this will mean deciding what kind of computer hardware and software you'll need for your particular project.

If all your sources are on one medium, it may be feasible to simply transfer them from the playback machine directly to your computer with no other equipment. However, if your source recordings reside on several different media requiring several types of playback equipment (some of which may be highly specialised), it might be more efficient to make an interim stage where the source materials are gathered together in a single format. This way any acoustic sound capture requiring specialist resources can be done in one go (such as a single recording studio session), whilst transfer of the sound to computer can be done in a less resource intensive way. For instance, if some of your sources are gramophone records requiring the use of a recording studio whilst the rest are on vinyl LPs, it makes sense to use one studio session to do all the gramophone capture but to do the LP digitisation elsewhere.

5.1. DAT

Any such interim stage may involve transfer of sources to DAT, digital audio tape (or to some other removable digital medium, such as ADAT). DAT uses magnetic tape to record digital information as outlined in section 3.5.1. The tape is housed inside a cassette, which though convenient is actually very delicate; one of the disadvantages of DAT is that it is not particularly rugged and can be susceptible to mechanical failure. The main advantage of DAT is that once sound is recorded, it is digitised: transfer to computer can be done via a digital link. See sections 7.3 and 7.4 for more information on digital transfers. If you do use DAT in this way, it is advisable to keep at least one backup version of the tape in case of failure. DAT machines are fairly straightforward to use, though the user manual should always be read before using.

5.2. APPLE MACINTOSH

Apple Macintosh (abbreviated to 'Mac') computers are very widely used in the digital audio world as they have built-in audio hardware and an internal architecture which is efficient at handling audio information.

This built-in audio hardware is probably sufficient for many basic digitisation tasks, though it does not allow for direct digital transfers, such as from DAT. The *G4* and *iMac* models can digitise audio at 16-bit resolution, 44.1kHz, and in stereo. However, for professional quality digitisation, it is best to invest in extra audio hardware which can be added to the computer. Such hardware would not be made by Apple but by specialist audio companies, and would be connected to the computer via either a *PCI* or a *USB* port.

Some professional level hardware comes bundled with software in the form of a sound editor, mixer and processor programme. One of the most widely used programmes is ProTools, made by Digidesign, which comes bundled with Digidesign audio hardware in various configurations. Some audio hardware may only support digital transfers, rather than digitisation from analogue sources. It is important to check manufacturers' specifications carefully before buying. See also section 5.6 on soundcards below.

5.3. PC: MICROSOFT WINDOWS

Microsoft Windows is an *operating system* widely used on IBM-compatible PC computers. PCs are made by many different companies and their technical specification can vary a great deal. The situation with regard to audio on PCs is somewhat complex as a result. PCs are usually purchased with some built-in audio support provided by a *soundcard*. Usually these soundcards are designed for game-playing or 'multimedia' (i.e. basic listening capability), and as such are generally unsuitable for professional audio work.

There are various options here: either a PC can be bought 'off the shelf', and the low-quality soundcard replaced by one purchased from a specialist dealer, or a PC can be ordered from certain manufacturers to one's own specification. It is important to note, though, that general PC manufacturers will not usually supply professional audio hardware. In this case it is probably best to order a PC with no sound capability, and then to purchase and fit the soundcard yourself. This will take a certain amount of technical expertise.

Some relatively low-cost soundcards may be suitable for digitisation purposes. See section 5.6 below.

In terms of other hardware specifications for a PC for digitising audio, the main considerations are the amount of RAM (computer memory: at least 128 megabytes is best); the amount of hard disk storage space (stereo, full bandwidth, or full resolution, digital audio takes up about 10 megabytes per minute, so for an hour's worth of sound that's 600 megabytes; you'll also need much more space than this for any post-digitisation work); the speed of the hard disk drive (if there is lots of audio, a fast disk with a speed of 7200 or 10000rpm will help); and the speed and efficiency of the processor/motherboard combination (a processor running at a minimum of 300MHz is recommended, and different types of processor will give different audio performance).

On the operating system side it is important to note that Windows exists in several versions: Windows 95 and Windows 98 have better support for audio hardware than Windows NT and Windows 2000. Audio under Windows NT can be difficult to get working, even if a particular soundcard purports to be 'compatible' with it.

There is a selection of software suitable for digitising audio under Windows, and programmes such as Syntrillium's CoolEditPro or Sonic Foundry's SoundForge offer a wide selection of post-digitisation processing. Note that the ProTools system is also available for PC, although it requires a very tightly specified hardware configuration.

5.4. PC: LINUX

Microsoft Windows is not the only operating system for PCs. *Linux* is a version of the *Unix* operating system that runs on PC. It has an advantage over other operating systems in that it is free, as is most of the software available for it.

However, audio support under Linux can be confusing, and is not comprehensive. There are two systems of audio support, called OSS (open sound system) and ALSA (Advanced Linux Sound Architecture). An increasing number of soundcards is being supported by both, but support for high-end hardware is patchy at present. There is also no single piece of software for Linux offering ease of use, flexibility and robustness comparable to those for the Mac or Windows systems.

5.5. PC: BEOS

BeOS is one of several other operating systems which run on the PC. It is optimised for digital media, so it's handling of sound and images is efficient. However, as with Linux only a small selection of hardware is supported at present.

5.6. WHAT TO LOOK FOR IN A SOUNDCARD

There are some computer audio solutions which are better established than others, as discussed above. If an 'off the shelf' professional audio bundle is not an option, maybe due to cost constraints, then it is important to know what to look for in the technical specification of audio hardware. Here is an outline of the basics.

Necessary connections:
    Line Input – for connection to the analogue playback device
    Line Output – for connection to a monitoring system (headphones or loudspeakers)
    These may be generically called *analogue input and output.*

    Digital Input – only necessary if digital transfer is required. This will usually be of the S/PDIF type.

In general, lower cost hardware will use *mini-jack* connectors for analogue input/output and *RCA phono* connectors for S/PDIF digital input/output (AES/EBU digital is usually via XLR connectors). On professional multi-channel cards, digital connections may be provided via TOSLINK, an optical interface. Some cards come with a *break-out box*, which may provide more robust connections.

Look in detail at the technical specification of the ADC and DAC (the *converters)*: look for *signal-to-noise ratios (S/N)* of at least 96dB (*decibels*), and a resolution of at least 16-bits. Some converters will offer higher resolutions of 20 or 24 bits.

Check that the card is fully supported under your hardware platform and operating system: this is especially pertinent if using Linux, Be, or Windows NT. In general for lower end audio hardware, it is not sufficient to trust manufacturers' claims about compatibility. It is best to find and join appropriate mailing lists and newsgroups prior to purchase. Some budget soundcards may have automatic recording level controls or volume controls; it is important to be aware of these and how to disable them.

Some professional level audio hardware may have multiple channels. This is superfluous unless you are digitising multitrack media. Some cards may not have analogue input/output at all, but may only support digital transfer – analogue input/output is essential if digitising direct from analogue sources.

5.7. CONNECTIONS AND ADDITIONAL EQUIPMENT

This section outlines the kind of connections that will need to be made between the playback equipment and the computer.

Open reel tape

> Line Output on the tape machine is usually via stereo phono or XLR connectors. These connect to the Line Input on the computer. There may be a playback volume control on the tape machine, which should be set using a test-tape and level meter (this may require specialist skills).

Cassette

> Line Output (or playback output) is usually via stereo phono connectors. These connect to Line Input on the computer. The playback level is usually factory-preset.

Records

> Turntable outputs are usually not at standard 'line' level, and cannot be directly connected to the computer; a suitable turntable pre-amplifier will be needed. Many domestic hi-fi amplifiers will do the job: connect the turntable to the Phono Input on the amplifier, then connect Line or Tape Output on the amplifier to Line Input on the computer. Select the phono input on the amplifier's front panel controls.

Gramophone & phonograph

> These acoustic machines require a microphone setup, preferably in an acoustically dry and quiet space such as a recording studio. It is best to seek specialist advice before handling such media and playback equipment.

Video

> VHS, S-VHS, U-matic, and Betacam video machines should have stereo Line Outputs for their audio signal. Some VHS machines may have 'Hi-Fi' audio output, which should be used if available. Some machines will provide audio signals via phono connectors, whilst others will have a multi-pin SCART socket. Other formats, such as D1, D2, D3, Hi8, Sony Digital Beta etc. carry digital audio tracks. It is important to use audio hardware which can support the correct type of digital audio signal.

Film

> Digitising film soundtracks will require detailed knowledge of the way audio tracks work for the particular format concerned. Different formats have used different numbers and types of audio tracks. Some have used stereo sound (e.g. Dolby Stereo), whilst others have used multiple channels for 'surround sound' cinema presentation (such as Dolby Six

Track, Cinemascope, Dolby Digital). Some modern formats use digital audio (such as Dolby Digital and DTS), whilst older formats use analogue (such as Dolby Stereo and Cinemascope). It is best to seek specialist advice if digitisation direct from film soundtracks is necessary.

5.8. STORING THE SOUND

As each audio sample is digitised, it will need to be stored on the computer's hard disk. Most software allows you to do this by selecting 'save' from a 'file' menu. Your sound will then be transferred from the computer's memory (which is cleared when you close down the programme, log out, or switch off the computer) onto the hard disk (a magnetic medium that holds data when the computer is switched off or used for other tasks). When you want to access the sound again (maybe to play or edit it) it is read back into memory from disk. For very long sounds, there may not be enough computer memory to hold the entire sound; in that case, the sound is read in from the disk in chunks as it is needed. So when dealing with long sounds, it may be that the computer needs to access the disk often; for this reason, it is best to have a high-performance (i.e. fast access) hard disk when dealing with samples of long duration. Hard disk performance can be measured in access time for read and write operations, and is generally better for disks with higher speeds of rotation. It is worth paying for hard disk performance if there is lots of audio to process.

Though storage of data on hard disk is generally reliable and fairly long term, it is not permanent and is still susceptible to mechanical and electrical failure. As a result, you should have way of backing up your audio files as you create them. You should also have a strategy for backing up and restoring all your data for the long term. Chapter 10 deals with these issues.

6. Other resources: skills and time

In addition to equipment, you will need particular skills if you are attempting audio digitisation yourself. Some of these skills have already been mentioned, and are summarised below. You will also need to allow enough time for the digitisation project; factors influencing the duration of the project are also summarised below.

It may be that your organisation has staff who can assist in the project, but they will need advance warning and large or specialised projects may need special arrangements to be made. If such staff are not available, it may be necessary to employ someone, or to approach external agencies or companies.

6.1. SKILLS SUMMARY

An audio digitisation project will involve the following activities:

- Negotiating copyright licence agreements
- Playback of original audio media
  ranging from setting up basic hi-fi equipment, to finding and acquiring suitable equipment for playing back film soundtracks, gramophone records, open reel tapes etc.
- Sound recording
  setting up recording sessions for mechanical media such as gramophones and phonographs.
- Audio sampling and storing
  researching available hardware platforms and software; setting up the computer; setting up audio interconnections to playback equipment and mixing desk; installing audio software; learning how to use software and hardware.
- Documentation, design and management
  documenting the sound files; incorporating them into the digital resource; presenting audio to the user; web site design.

6.2. FACTORS INFLUENCING PROJECT DURATION

- Research time

finding and obtaining audio source materials; obtaining copyright clearance for materials (bearing in mind other recordings will need to be found if licences are refused).

- Preparation time
  setting up equipment; familiarisation with new software or hardware; preparing source materials for digitisation.

- Capture time
  time for playing, converting and storing the recordings. It is crucial to realise that this can take much longer than the total duration of sound you have. The time requirement will depend very much on each individual case: for example, lots of brief sound recordings may take longer to digitise than a few long ones. Allow time for mistakes, level adjustments etc.

- Storage time
  saving audio to disk; backing up digital files.

- Post-processing time
  editing; applying noise reduction if necessary; saving edited files.

- Organisation time
  arranging files within the resource.

- Documentation time
  preparing documentation; entering data.

7. Creating digital audio files: a step-by-step guide

Before embarking on the digitisation itself, you should have planned the project thoroughly, sourced all the necessary resources, and obtained, set up and tested your equipment. You should also have familiarised yourself with any equipment or software which is new to you.

Once you are at this stage, you are ready to prepare for the recording process itself. This will involve setting up audio connections for recording and listening, and organising source materials to make the process hassle-free.

7.1. FINAL PREPARATIONS

7.1.1. Setting up audio connections

The connections you need to make will depend on the type and combination of media you have.

- For a single analogue source medium: connect the playback machine directly to the computer's audio input.
- For multiple analogue media: either switch between playback machines, plugging each type into the computer in turn, or use a mixing console; each machine connects to the mixer inputs, and the stereo output of the mixer connects to the computer audio input. It is usually advisable to use a suitable mixer rather than constantly plugging and unplugging devices.
- For a combination of digital and analogue media: the digital machine (e.g. DAT) can remain connected to the audio hardware independently of the analogue machines. There will be a way of selecting either the digital or the analogue input in the computer software. On the PC, this is usually a software 'mixer' programme, on the Mac this is usually done from an 'audio settings' type option from one of the sound editor programme's drop-down menus.

7.1.2. Monitoring

It is important to be able to hear what is going on throughout the digitisation process. You need to be able to hear the playback of your sources so that you can identify the audio segments you want to digitise; you also need to hear the output of the computer, so that you can listen back to the digitised sounds and check them.

This is called *monitoring*, and it can be done using either loudspeakers or headphones. Whichever is used, use good quality equipment to ensure accurate aural feedback.

In order to monitor effectively it is necessary to work in a quiet environment environment – this may mean situating your monitoring away from the computer itself. One of the less desirable features of working with computer audio is the noise of computer disks and fans. Some computers are quieter than others, and individual machines of the same type can differ in the perceived intrusiveness of the noise they make. You may wish to take this into account when sourcing equipment.

To set up monitoring, the analogue line output of the computer's audio hardware is used. When you play back a sound which has already been digitised, the computer sends it out through this connector. The hardware should also be able to pass sound from its input through to this output; that means you should be able to monitor sound coming from the playback machine through this output of the computer. To do this, you may need to enable *input monitor* or something similar on your computer's audio mixer or sound editor programme. This will effectively send the input signal straight to the output. The advantage of this is that you only need to connect your monitor loudspeakers or headphones to the output of the computer; you need not connect them to the outputs of your playback machines at all.

The analogue line output of your audio hardware should be connected to your headphones or loudspeakers. Some soundcards (usually low-end cards) allow the direct connection of headphones to this socket, others don't. If your soundcard doesn't, you'll need to connect it to an amplifier and then use the headphone socket on the amplifier. If you are using loudspeakers, you should use a high quality pair in conjunction with any necessary amplification. A good quality domestic hi-fi amplifier and speakers should be sufficient. It is unlikely that purpose made 'PC speakers' will be of sufficient quality to provide adequate monitoring accuracy, except in the most basic of digitisation projects.

7.1.3. Organising the process

Once your playback and monitoring equipment is connected to the computer, you can organise your source materials so that the recording process flows efficiently.

- Make a list of the source materials, in the order of digitisation, and with timings if necessary.
- Minimise changing of media; deal with sources of a common medium consecutively.
- Know what format you are going to use for digitisation: decide on sampling rate, resolution, and sound file format. These are covered in section 3.5.2 and below.

7.2. RECORDING FROM ANALOGUE SOURCES

1   Select the Line or Analogue input on the computer's audio mixer, audio control panel, or from the audio options menu item. It may be that your hardware lets you record from more than one source at a time; many lower end soundcards have a microphone input in addition to the line input, and may have 'virtual' inputs from MIDI synthesisers etc. Make sure none of these other sources are selected, or you will be recording extra noise from these inputs along with the sound you want.

2   Set the appropriate sampling rate, resolution etc on the computer. Some soundcards allow

the adjustment of these, in which case there will usually be an option in the audio mixer or sound editor software for doing so. At the digitisation stage, it is best to choose full bandwidth and full resolution. Full bandwidth means using a sampling rate of 44.1 kHz or above, and full resolution means using at least 16-bit sampling. 24-bit sampling will result in a more dynamic and vivid reproduction, but in general only professional level audio hardware will support this. Even if the sounds are to be used in a low-bandwidth situation (such as streaming over the Internet), it is worth making full bandwidth originals. Though they take up more disk space, you can downgrade them later. Low bandwidth originals can never be upgraded to produce clearer sounds.

3   Adjust the recording levels. To do this, you should use a test tape, test cassette or test disc. These contain accurately recorded test signals (usually sine tones) at a specific reference level, which you can use to calibrate your audio hardware. Normally test tones will be recorded at a level of 0 dB (decibels), so you should play the test tone and check the level meters on the computer. These are usually found in the mixer panel or in the audio settings control panel. Adjust the computer's record level control until the level meters read 0 dB, the same as the recorded tone on tape or disc. You should always try to use test tones to calibrate record levels. If not, you will need to playback your source recording and adjust the levels, aiming toward an average level of around –12 dB (usually about two-thirds of the way up the scale) and a peak level just below 0 dB at the top. Be aware that with a digital audio system, if the signal rises above the 0 dB mark it will distort, almost certainly resulting in audible clicks or crackling, (called *clipping*).

If you are using a professional system, the audio hardware may already be calibrated to a reference level. If this is the case you should be using a mixing desk in conjunction with the computer, because if the source recording is at a non-standard level or was poorly recorded, you will need to increase its playback volume. A mixing desk will allow you to do this.

4   Create a new sound file using the sound editor. This is usually available from a 'File' menu, and at this point you may be asked to define the sampling rate, number of channels (i.e. stereo or mono), and possibly how long the file should be in seconds. The settings you choose here should correspond to those of the audio hardware made in step 2, otherwise your sound may playback at the incorrect speed and pitch.

5   Click on the record button of your sound editor, and the recording should begin. Then start the playback of your source sound. You should see some indication of fluctuating levels as the volume of your source varies.

6   When the end of your source sound is reached, stop the playback machine. Then, click on the stop button of your sound editor. Doing things this way round means you won't accidentally miss the beginning or end of your sound. The rule is: press record on the computer, then play on the other machine; press stop on the machine, then stop on the computer. There will be a silent gap at the beginning and end of the sound file, but this is ok: it can be removed later.

7   Immediately do a quick check that your sound has recorded. Return your sound editor to the beginning of the sound, and click on the playback button. If your monitoring is set up

correctly, you should hear your sound playback perfectly. If not, you need to check your audio settings and connections.

8   Save your sound file to the computer's hard disk. The 'Save' option is usually under the 'File' menu. Name your file something identifiable, and choose a file format most commonly used for the platform you are on. Under MacOS, this will be AIFF (standard Audio Interchange File Format). Under Windows, this will be WAV (a Microsoft file format). Professional sound editors on either platform will be able to cope with both WAV and AIFF files. Other types of files may not be supported on different types of computer. Do not choose a file format with compression at this stage, because you may want to do some post-digitisation processing (see section 7.5 below), and this is best done on uncompressed sound data.

You are now ready to move on to the next sound. If your last sound was very long, it is probably best to 'Close' it from the 'File' menu. This will free up the computer memory that was holding it. You can then return to step 4, though you may need to reset levels as in step 3.

7.3. DIGITAL TRANSFERS FROM DAT

If your sound materials have been digitised onto DAT tape (or any other digital tape format) then all that needs to be done is to transfer them to computer. Digital transfers are much easier than analogue transfers, as no recording levels need be set and there are no potential sources of background noise. However, it is important to be aware that digital errors can occur in such transfers, for a variety of reasons, which could result in clicks, dropouts or other noises occurring in the audio file.

Making a digital transfer from a DAT machine to a computer's audio hardware is simply a case of connecting an appropriate cable from the S/PDIF or AES/EBU output of the DAT, to the digital input of the computer. Using cables of high quality and avoiding excessive length (a few metres maximum) should help to avoid errors. In established sound studios or editing suites such connections should already be in place (as should analogue connections).

When making the recording, you will need to select the 'Digital' input of the computer's audio hardware. This may be found in the mixer panel, or in an audio options menu in the audio recording software you are using. There may be other settings which you need to make, and you should consult the manuals for your particular software and hardware.

7.4. DIGITAL EXTRACTION FROM AUDIO CD

Some audio CD players have a digital signal output, in which case sound can be transferred digitally to the computer in the same way as for DAT above. In addition, most modern computer CD-ROM drives are capable of extracting audio tracks from CDs and placing them straight into audio files, using data transfer which is completely internal to the computer. There are many software products capable of doing this, including many CD-burning programmes.

7.5. POST-DIGITISATION TASKS

Once you have digitised your sounds, you will almost certainly need to do some post-digitisation processing. The most common operations will be:

- Editing out unwanted segments of sound, such as silence at the beginning and end. 'Zooming in' on the sound can assist in finding appropriate points at which to make edits. You may also wish to apply a short fade to avoid clicks at these points, or your sound editor may be configured to do this automatically.

- Removing hiss, clicks and pops, rumble, and pitched hum. Advanced sound editors sometimes have functions for doing this, either built in or as optional *plug-ins* which can be purchased separately. Refer to user manuals and help files for information on how to use them. Some will be more useful than others for particular sounds, and bear in mind that they will result in changing the spectral content of the sound, possibly significantly. For instance, de-clicking may lead to some loss of clarity of attack transients in musical material. For very noisy sources, a significant degree of trial and error and careful listening will be required; it may be that in extreme cases, so much processing is required to make a sound seem 'clean' that much of the desired sound has been eradicated. If this happens, it may be better just to leave the sound in its noisy state. The intended use of the digitised sound will also have a bearing on how much cleaning up is necessary or desirable.

- Converting sound files into compressed or streamable formats. As they stand your sound files are good copies of the originals, but are cumbersome for delivery over the Internet. In order to reduce the time taken to download them, the sound file data can be compressed. Alternatively, they may be converted into a format which can be streamed in real-time over the Internet. This area is covered in more detail in chapter 9.

8. Documenting digital audio resources

8.1. INTRODUCTION

Whether you are creating a small number of digital audio files as an individual project, or developing a larger collection, it is crucial to document key information about each digital object, or group of objects. Without this information it may be impossible for others to identify the *content* of the audio resource (e.g. the composer, the title of the work, the performer(s)), for users to *access* the work (e.g. information about file size, encoding standards or software), or for you to *manage* the project on a long-term basis (e.g. information about copyright or data preservation strategies).

In the digital environment, we call this information *metadata* (or 'data about data') and it may include the kind of information found in a library catalogue record, a listing in the *Radio Times*, or in the booklet of a CD.

This information can be used to support a number of different activities:

- **Resource location/finding** – without a description of the content of your resource, potential users may not be able to find it!

- **Resource access and use** – once users have found your resource they will need to know about the format (including file type and data size) in order to listen to it. They may also need to know about access or re-use restrictions due to copyright or other considerations.

- **Resource management** – in many cases, information relating to the resource must be stored for administrative purposes. This may include the name and address of the copyright holders, the location of analogue originals or surrogates of the resource or details of the staff members responsible for the project.

- **E-commerce** – if you hope to charge for your resource it will be necessary to include information about charging levels and other restrictions.

- **Digital Preservation** – without information about the format and file size of the resource, details of its original encoding and of any subsequent re-encoding or migration to new software it will prove increasingly difficult to preserve the resource for future use.

Creating metadata can be as simple or as complicated as the project requires. Information professionals working in libraries or archives are all too aware that cataloguing their resources can be time-consuming and costly. The decisions you make about documenting your digital collection can significantly alter the duration and cost of your project and these issues should be addressed before a single audio resource is encoded.

Metadata is still in its infancy and will undoubtedly undergo a long process of evolution. This chapter cannot hope to pre-empt that development by offering a simple solution to the problem of creating appropriate documentation. What is clear, however, is that best practice *now* can save precious time and resources at a later date as standards emerge. Equally, issues that have exercised music and audio-visual librarians and archivists in the analogue world are just as pertinent in the digital one and must be addressed by a new community of digital resource creators.

Although this Guide to Good Practice is intended as a 'How To', covering all aspects of digital resource creation, this chapter does not attempt to evaluate different modes of creating or storing metadata from a technical perspective. The range of skills, resources and institutional support available to data creation projects varies enormously. Most projects will create and store metadata in a database. Some will develop metadata using XML or a similar mark-up language. For more information please see the bibliography.

8.2. DEVELOPING METADATA – UNDERSTANDING THE ENVIRONMENT

In order to develop appropriate documentation for your digital resource, you should first consider the environment in which your resource is created and those environments in which it will be used and where it may be accessible in the future:

8.2.1. Identifying the needs of your primary user group(s)

Collections of digital objects are most often designed to enhance access to otherwise inaccessible analogue collections (although increasingly resources may be 'born digital' – that is, they may have no analogue original). In either case, users will have a variety of different needs which your metadata should seek to incorporate.

What information do these users need in order to obtain the best possible value from your resource?

8.2.2. Identifying the potential for further re-use of your data

Although you may be creating your data for a specific user group with specialised needs, you should be aware of the potential for new uses in the future. For example:

- your institution may be part of a consortium of similar archives and libraries who may wish to create a union catalogue of their digital and analogue holdings

- your university department may wish to make searchable records of its digital projects available alongside others in the humanities faculty

- you may eventually deposit copies of your resources with a UK-wide service such as the Arts and Humanities Data Service

8.2.3. Understanding the local environment

Creating metadata can be expensive and time-consuming and depend on specialised skills. The complexity of your metadata will ultimately depend on the skills and resources available to your project. Access to specialist librarian or archival skills can be enormously valuable, but creating simple metadata structures, following basic rules, is an achievable goal for all data creators.

8.3. WHAT INFORMATION SHOULD BE INCLUDED IN MY RECORD?

In 1988, at their Annual Conference in Vienna, the International Association of Sound Archives Discography/Cataloguing Working Group presented their recommended list of data elements required for describing recorded sound events.

IASA recommended list of data elements for cataloguing sound recordings

Title
Programme Title
Series Title
Uniform Title
Names (incl. types of 'functions' related to those names)
– Composer
– Author
– Librettist
– Artist
– Orchestra
Medium of performance (e.g. Violin)
Name of Broadcasting Service/Station
– Name of Broadcaster
Other information related to names:
Voice (e.g. Soprano)
– Character/Role (e.g. Aida)
Contents listing (e.g. list of track on an LP)
Summary (e.g. Synopsis of text/interview)
Language
Label
Catalogue Number
Matrix Number
Shelf Location
Location of other copies
Physical Description
– Format (e.g. disc, tape, etc)
– Speed
– Size
– Mono/Stereo
– Analogue (recording)

- – Digital (recording
- – Analogue (mix)
- – Digital (mix)
- – Analogue (replay)
- – Digital (replay)

Duration

Technical Quality

- – Sound quality
- – Physical Condition

Place of Recording

Recording Date

Broadcast Date (first date of broadcast)

Copyright holder

Embargo

Copyright

Royalties

Obligations accruing from acquiring the recording

Date of Entry

Name of Person who entered the entry to the system

Although these data elements are intended primarily for analogue resources, the information your users need to access and understand your data resources will be similar. (It should be noted that these fields are not intended to be mandatory and that the words 'if applicable', 'if readily available' and 'as appropriate' follow many of the data elements in the list).

8.4. UNDERSTANDING THE STATUS OF YOUR METADATA RECORD – WHAT ARE YOU DESCRIBING?

Now you have an idea of the kind of information that users may need, but in order to develop an appropriate *structure* for your metadata it is important to identify the concepts, items and events that you wish to document.

This can be a complex procedure, as it is often intimately bound up with the way that you and your users understand the meaning and relationships between a performance and its many manifestations.

Just as a metadata record can be seen as a surrogate for a digital object – providing information about the intellectual content of a resource – so the object that you are documenting is also likely to be a surrogate. Listening to a recording of a concert can be seen as a surrogate for the experience of attending that concert, for example.

Your recording may be one of several clips from a single piece of music or oral history interview and should be approached as part of a sequence. The relationship between each object, and to any parent object, should therefore also be documented

The Digital Music Library Initiative at Indiana University (http://www.dml.indiana.edu/metadata/) has identified five primary categories of information for music resources that may provide a useful structure for creating and linking metadata records that document different, but related, concepts:

- **Work**

  A musical Work is an abstract thing; it should not be confused with a performance, recording, score, or otherwise physical *Instantiation* of that Work. Beethoven's 5th Symphony is a musical Work, and we would associate with it a composer, composition date, and other data pertaining to the Work itself.

- **Collective Work**

  Collective Works bring together multiple Works that share some information in common. The Brandenburg concerti are an example of a Collective Work – while they were not written as a unit, they were collected together as a unit. Likewise, Beethoven's nine symphonies could be viewed as a collection of musical Works.

- **Instantiations**

  An instantiation is a manifestation of a Work. A recording of Beethoven's 5th Symphony is an Instance of that Work, as is a musical score of the same Work.

- **Containers**

  Instances of a Work must be brought together somewhere; CDs, LPs, anthologies of scores, and other similar physical entities are Containers. A CD contains on it (potentially) many Instances of many different Works (a typical CD of pop music); similarly, it may contain only one or part of one Instance of a very long Work (as is the case with many operas).

- **Name**

  Composers, performers, choirs, quartets – all of these individuals and groups that contribute to the making of a Work, Instance, or Container are represented by a Name record.

Each of these record types is capable of supporting links to other records, sometimes of the same type, sometimes of differing types. For example, a Work record might link to a Name record belonging to the composer of that Work.

A similar set of record types may also be identified for recordings of theatrical performances, oral history interviews, and other recordings.

8.5. USING STANDARDS

We have looked at the kind of information that users are likely to require and started to understand that there are many levels of data and different relationships between events and recordings and between digital resources and their analogue surrogates.

In order to create a working system of documentation, you must also address the issue of *standards*.

There are two types of standard that you must address in creating your documentation. Broadly speaking, standards fall into the following categories:

- **Integrity or authority standards**

  These are the rules developed by library and archive professionals to facilitate effective information retrieval. These standards may include agreed proper forms for personal names (e.g. Tchaikovsky rather than Chaykovsky) or internationally-agreed ways of expressing dates.

- **Frameworks**

  When we talk about metadata standards we usually mean the frameworks that have been developed to store separate pieces of information – equivalent to the individual fields in a database. These will include the types of information recommended by the International Association of Sound Archives (see Section 8.4) but will often be grouped in a certain way and use general, non subject-specific terms (for example, CREATOR instead of COMPOSER)

8.5.1. Why should we use standards?

Standards improve understanding of a resource. Without standard names (usually with dates of birth and death attached) we do not know whether you mean *that* John Smith, or another John Smith altogether. Without standardised date forms (1999/07/05), American (07/05/1999) and European (05/07/1999) users will become quickly confused.

Standards facilitate intuitive searching of a resource. Without standardised terminology to describe the content, genre or category of a resource, users cannot find resources effectively.

8.5.2. Which standards?

Standards for data entry – authority, integrity and consistency

Even if you are creating an extremely basic record, it is important to understand the impact of your data entry methodologies. If you only follow one rule as a data creator, that rule must be *consistency*.

Names, dates and titles

Since 1967, most UK and US libraries have been using the *Anglo-American Cataloguing Rules* to describe the items in their collections. Use of AACR as the common standard for cataloguing has made it possible for libraries to pool their efforts through the use of derived cataloguing and shared cataloguing projects. Of equal importance, the adoption of AACR has provided consistency and clarity for library users. Although the rules are in perpetual revision, the basic principles for best practice remain broadly constant. AACR2 (Anglo-American cataloguing rules, 2nd ed. 1988 revision) provides building blocks for the construction of meaningful and consistent data entries for names, dates and titles and other information, including format(s).

For example, the standard form for personal names is as follows:

Bach, Johann Sebastian, 1685–1750

Note that the forenames and surname order is inverted and that the dates of birth and death are incorporated (so that we know *which* Johann Sebastian Bach).

Musical works often have multiple titles and may also be known by their numbers (e.g. Symphony Number 9). Chapter 8 of the Anglo-American Cataloguing Rules offers a formula for constructing a *uniform* title which incorporates all the appropriate information in a recognised form:

> Sehet, welch eine Liebe hat uns der Vater erzeiget = See now, what kind of love this is : BWV64 / Bach, Johann Sebastian, 1685–1750. 1982

The uniform title above includes the full title of the Cantata in German, the English translation of that title, the standard catalogue number for the work, derived from W. Schmieder's reference work 'Thematisch-systematisches Verzeichnis der musikalischen Werke' and the full names and dates of the composer.

Subjects and classification

Most libraries group similar resources together under headings, or use classification schemes such as Dewey Decimal classification scheme, the Universal Decimal Classification scheme (UDC) or the Library of Congress classification scheme (LC). As well as directing users to a particular section of a physical library space, these schemes also help users to find other items dealing with the same subjects or concepts. You may wish to incorporate a standard classification statement in your record to help users understand the context and meaning of your resource. For example, you may wish to assign your resource a Dewey Decimal classification number. Many audio resources may fall under the following categories:

> 780 Music
> 781 General principles & musical forms
> 782 Vocal music
> 783 Music for single voices
> 784 Instruments & Instrumental ensembles
> 785 Chamber music
> 786 Keyboard & other instruments
> 787 Stringed instruments
> 788 Wind instruments

Most resources will be assigned further refinements:

> 780 Music: general resources
> 780 Music: departments and institutions
> 780 Music: education and research
> 780 Music: journals and magazines
> 780 Music: libraries
> 780 Music: collections
> 780.285 Music software
> 780.82 Women in music
> 780.89 Ethnomusicology
> 780.9 Music of specific areas
> 780.9 Music of specific periods
> 780.92 Composers
> 781 General principles and traditions of music
> 782 Vocal music
> 782.1 Opera

784 Orchestral and instrumental ensembles and their music
784.19 Musical instruments: general resources
786 Keyboard and percussion instruments
787 Stringed instruments
788 Wind instruments
788.9 Brass instruments

Some non-music resources may be categorised as follows:

791 Public performances
- 791.028 Acting
- 791.43028 Film actors/actresses
- 791.4309 History of film
- 791.437 Screenplays
- 791.44 Radio
- 791.45 Television

792 Stage presentations; Theatre
- 792.027 Stage makeup
- 792.09 History of theatre
- 792.3 Mime

8.6. METADATA STANDARDS – DUBLIN CORE (DC) AND THE RESOURCE DISCOVERY FRAMEWORK (RDF)

8.6.1. Interoperability

Metadata standards are fundamentally about interoperability, or in other words, they allow users to search your resources alongside resources created by other people, in different institutions, at different times and covering different subject areas. This is still an emerging area in the study of digital resources and their usage and there are no definitive guidelines for structuring all forms of data appropriately. Metadata standards therefore inevitably come in a variety of 'flavours'. However, the fundamental aim of those agencies developing standards for describing digital resources is *resource discovery* in an environment where the proliferation of data on the Internet and elsewhere is becoming increasingly problematic.

8.6.2 The Dublin Core Metadata Set

The Dublin Core Metadata Initiative (DCMI) is an open forum engaged in the development of interoperable online metadata standards. The DCMI have devised a 'core' set of 15 metadata elements (or fields) which can be used to create simple descriptions of digital resources.

Element: Title	**Definition**:A name given to the resource. **Comment**:Typically, a Title will be a name by which the resource is formally known.
Element: Creator	**Definition**:An entity primarily responsible for making the content of the resource. **Comment**:Examples of a Creator include a person, an organisation, or a service.
Element: Subject	**Definition**:The topic of the content of the resource. **Comment**:Typically, a Subject will be expressed as keywords, key phrases or classification codes that describe a topic of the resource. Recommended best practice is to select a value from a controlled vocabulary or formal classification scheme.
Element: Description	**Definition**:An account of the content of the resource. **Comment**:Description may include but is not limited to: an abstract, table of contents, reference to a graphical representation of content or a free-text account of the content.
Element: Publisher	**Definition**:An entity responsible for making the resource available **Comment**:Examples of a Publisher include a person, an organisation, or a service.
Element: Contributor	**Definition**:An entity responsible for making contributions to the content of the resource. **Comment**:Examples of a Contributor include a person, an organisation, or a service.
Element: Date	**Definition**: A date associated with an event in the life cycle of the resource. **Comment**: Typically, Date will be associated with the creation or availability of the resource. Recommended best practice for encoding the date value is defined in a profile of ISO 8601 and follows the YYYY-MM-DD format.
Element: Type	**Definition**:The nature or genre of the content of the resource. **Comment**: Type includes terms describing general categories, functions, genres, or aggregation levels for content. Recommended best practice is to select a value from a controlled vocabulary.
Element: Format	**Definition**:The physical or digital manifestation of the resource. **Comment**:Typically, Format may include the media-type or dimensions of the resource. Format may be used to determine the software, hardware or other equipment needed to display or operate the resource. Examples of dimensions include size and

	duration. Recommended best practice is to select a value from a controlled vocabulary (for example, the list of Internet Media-Types defining computer media formats).
Element: Identifier	**Definition**:An unambiguous reference to the resource within a given context. **Comment**:Recommended best practice is to identify the resource by means of a string or number conforming to a formal identification system. Example formal identification systems include the Uniform Resource Identifier (URI), the Digital Object Identifier (DOI) and the International Standard Book Number (ISBN).
Element: Source	**Definition**:A reference to a resource from which the present resource is derived. **Comment**:The present resource may be derived from the Source resource in whole or in part. Recommended best practice is to reference the resource by means of a string or number conforming to a formal identification system.
Element: Language	**Definition**:A language of the intellectual content of the resource. **Comment**:Recommended best practice for the values of the Language element is defined by RFC 1766 [RFC1766] which includes a two-letter Language Code (taken from the ISO 639 standard [ISO639]), followed optionally, by a two-letter Country Code (taken from the ISO 3166 standard [ISO3166]). For example, 'en' for English, 'fr' for French, or 'en-uk' for English used in the United Kingdom.
Element: Relation	**Definition**:A reference to a related resource. **Comment**:Recommended best practice is to reference the resource by means of a string or number conforming to a formal identification system.
Element: Coverage	**Definition**:The extent or scope of the content of the resource. **Comment**:Coverage will typically include spatial location (a place name or geographic co-ordinates), temporal period (a period label, date, or date range).
Element: Rights	**Definition**:Information about rights held in and over the resource. **Comment**:Typically, a Rights element will contain a rights management statement for the resource, or reference a service providing such information. Rights information often encompasses Intellectual Property Rights (IPR), Copyright, and various Property Rights.

The Dublin Core set of metadata elements is intended primarily for *resource discovery* – or, in other words, is a tool for users to locate your resource and understand basic information about its content and status. The Dublin Core elements were designed to offer a simple, interoperable, framework for data creators who wish to provide information about their resources. The elements can be located by some search engines to contextualise search information and they are used to facilitate interoperable working by different individuals and organizations.

You may wish to create a basic Dublin Core record for each of your audio files. Or you may wish to create more complex records, perhaps based on the set of fields recommended by the IASA (above) and 'map' selected fields onto their Dublin Core counterpart.

8.6.3. Using existing data to create your documentation

If your project is digitising an existing collection of analogue resources there may be existing documentation which can adapted and extended to incorporate new data relating to the digital object. If you are working in a library or archival environment and catalogue materials using existing standards such as MARC, ISADG or EAD, researchers at the Getty Institute (http://www.getty.edu/research/institute/standards/intrometadata/index.html), at the Library of Congress (http://www.loc.gov/standards/metadata.html) or at UKOLN (http://www.ukoln.ac.uk/metadata/interoperability/) have devised 'crosswalks' or models for mapping existing cataloguing fields to metadata frameworks.

8.6.4. The Resource Discovery Framework and extending metadata structures

Increasingly, data creators are recognising that, although creating interoperable metadata is a vital way to share valuable resources, the documentation needed by an individual project to effectively manage its data may be far more complex and employ very specific language and syntax readily understandable only by a specialised audience.

The Resource Description Framework (RDF) – developed by the World Wide Web Consortium (W3C) – provides the foundation for metadata interoperability across different resource description communities. RDF supports a 'packaging' of different types of metadata in a single description by creating a framework for tagging each piece of data. Even though different elements may have been culled from different standards, by tagging each element it is possible to understand the content in the context of the original methodology.

A RDF/Dublin Core record for the online version of this Guide to Good Practice might look like this:

<?xml:namespace href="http://www.pads.ahds.ac.uk/GGP/ as="RDF"?> <?xml:namespace href=" http://www.pads.ahds.ac.uk/GGP as="DC"?> <RDF:RDF> <RDF:Description> <DC:Title>**Creating Digital Audio Resources**</DC:Title> <DC:Creator>**Catherine Owen**</DC:Creator> <DC:Creator>**Nick Fells**</DC:Creator> <DC:Creator>**Pauline Donachy**</DC:Creator> <DC:Subject>**digitisation, copyright, audio, metadata**</DC:Subject> <DC:Description>**This Guide describes the methodologies for creating, documenting and managing digital audio projects.**</DC:Description>

```
<DC:Publisher>Performing Arts Data Service<DC:Publisher>
<DC:Identifier>http://www.pads.ahds.ac.uk/GGP</DC:Identifier>
<DC:Format>text/html</DC:Format>
<DC:Type>technical guide</DC:Type>
<DC:Language>en</DC:Language>
<DC:Date>2001-08-30</DC:Date> </RDF:Description> </RDF:RDF>
```

8.7. CONCLUSION

In order to create an effective resource, which is accessible to different user groups, and easy to manage by you or your organisation, you must create documentation which describes the content and status of the resource and its constituent parts.

This documentation does not have to be complex, but it should be created with an understanding of the broader environment in which your resources are created. It is better to create a few, simple metadata elements that you can ensure are interoperable and to fill them with accessible and appropriately-structured information than to attempt a complex cataloguing project with no reference to existing standards.

The technology you use to store your metadata may also influence its structure. If you are working within an existing library or archival environment, you may wish to create metadata records for your objects in the cataloguing system used by that library. It is usually possible to export records to another format where they may be stored in a different structure if you wish to create interoperable metadata that has a broader application than merely part of a single institutional collection.

You may wish to use a standard database package such as Microsoft Access or FileMaker Pro, which can be easily programmed to store any form of metadata structure, or you may store your metadata as text in html or XML.

The most important rule for any documentation process is consistency. Once you make the decision to use a particular spelling, classification scheme or title convention you *must* always use the same rules for each record. Without internal consistency, your collection will be next to useless.

9. Presentation and delivery

How you want your audio presented to the user and how you want to incorporate it into the digital resource as a whole will determine the ultimate form of your digitised sounds. There are several ways in which you could deliver a digital resource, and within those there are various ways in which the audio itself can be delivered. Your resource may be on CD-ROM, an organisation's internal network (or Intranet), or the web (aka the Internet). These are discussed below.

9.1. CD-ROM

The benefits of delivering a digital resource via a CD-ROM are:

- access can be controlled easily. This may mean that copyright clearance is easier to negotiate, as the number of users can be carefully restricted.

- audio can be incorporated without needing to consider the operation of the resource over a network. Download time is not a factor, so the performance of your resource can be more easily assured: the delivery is independent of network conditions. This may also mean that full-bandwidth uncompressed sound can be used (for instance in the form of 'wav' files), achieving maximum sound quality.

The disadvantages are:

- CDs are a physical medium: they have production costs, they take up space, and they need to be physically delivered to users.

- they have limited storage capacity, so the amount of audio you can present is limited also.

- they cannot be updated once created. This limits the life span of the CD if the resource is likely to be subject to ongoing development or updating.

Materials presented on CD-ROM can be organised and constructed in the same way as web sites, or they can be presented as 'multimedia applications', effectively programmes which run when the CD is inserted into the computer. There are many tools (commercial and non-commercial) which assist with building both types of presentation. Some require a significant level of technical knowledge (in such areas as HTML programming, for instance), whereas others operate on a more intuitive *wysiwyg* (what you see is what you get) basis.

9.2. NETWORKS AND THE WEB

The advantages of presenting a resource via a network or the web are:

- The resource is highly accessible internationally (at least on the web).

- It is instantly updateable by the resource owner.

- There is effectively unlimited data capacity, though storage space obviously costs.

- It can link to other databases/resources.

- No physical media are involved in delivering the resource.

The disadvantages are:

- Resource performance is limited by network performance: sound files may need to be compressed and quality may be compromised.

- The resource requires ongoing technical support.

- Having open access will impinge on copyright negotiations; alternatively, a system of access control can be incorporated.

9.2.1. Delivering audio via networks and the web

There are two options for delivering audio files over networks (including the Internet/web):

- File download: the soundfile resides on a server computer belonging to the resource owner (quite possibly the same computer that hosts the web site itself). When a user clicks on a link to the sound in their web-browser, the whole file is sent from the server to the client (the user's computer). The user can usually choose to save the file to disk to play it later, or have their browser load it straight into a sound-player programme: in either case, the user will only be able to hear any sound at all once the entire file is downloaded.

- Streaming: again, the file resides on the resource owner's server. When the user clicks a link to the sound, this starts up a browser *plug-in* which downloads the file bit by bit, playing each bit as it goes (this is called *buffering*). The user starts to hear sound as soon as the first little bit of the file is received: usually after a second or two, no matter how long the entire file is. The plug-in will just keep receiving and playing until the end of the sound is reached. This method means the user does not have the option to save the whole file (i.e. to make a copy of it on their own computer's hard disk).

9.2.2. Data compression

With both these methods of audio data delivery, efficiency is dependent on the available network 'bandwidth'. If the network is fast, data can be sent more quickly than if it is slow. The speed of a network, including the Internet, varies with the amount of other use it is getting; UK access to the Internet, for example, slows down considerably when the USA 'wakes up', as there is much more network traffic. In order to minimise the problem of slow delivery, data compression is used.

There are various ways in which the size of any kind of digital data can be reduced. With audio data compression, there are types of compression which are 'lossy' and others which are 'lossless'. Lossy compression discards some data and retains that which is thought to be essential. Some very effective compression methods use lossy compression to achieve huge reductions in data size but with very good estimations of what our ears need to hear and what they don't. They use a detailed mapping of the responses of our hearing system as the basis for deciding what is essential data and what is redundant.

For the 'file download' method of delivery, using a compressed soundfile format can greatly reduce the time it takes to download the sound. Using modern data compression such as MPEG Layer III encoding (commonly known as 'mpeg 3' or 'mp3'), the size of a full-bandwidth soundfile can be reduced by as large a ratio as 10:1 or more, with little or no perceptible loss of quality. This results in a comparable reduction in download time. If some loss of quality is acceptable, and the file is converted to a lower bandwidth and mono, ratios of 200:1 can be achieved.

9.2.3. What difference does compression make?

To demonstrate this, we need to do some maths.

Standard WAV and AIFF format sound files (among others) do not generally use data compression. Every sound sample is stored as a numeric value – there is a sample value for every sample period, i.e. at a sampling rate of 44.1kHz 1 second of sound will generate 44100 sample values.

If these samples are stereo and are at 16-bit resolution, then each one will occupy 4 bytes of computer memory. So our 1 second sound will occupy 44100 x 4 = 176400 bytes. A minute of sound will occupy 10 584 000 bytes, or ca. 10 megabytes of memory or disk space.

Can we estimate how long it might take to download a file of this size via a modem over the Internet?

A modern modem might achieve a transfer rate of ca. 30kbps (kilobits per second). There are 8 bits per byte, so 1 minute of sound is 10 million x 8 = 80 million bits. 80 000 000 / 30 000 = 2666 seconds, or ca. 45 minutes.

But if we use a 10:1 compression ratio, this reduces to 4.5 minutes. Hence the attraction of data compression!

9.2.4. Streaming

Audio streaming depends on the server and network being able to supply enough data fast enough to the user's computer to enable it to play back the sound without audible gaps. The ability of the network to accomplish this is variable, especially where the Internet is concerned; at times of heavy traffic, congestion means that much less data can get through to any particular computer in a given time period. In order to get around this problem, audio streaming software uses a kind of data compression where the compression ratio can be varied. When network conditions are good, a lower ratio can be used, giving greater audio bandwidth and better quality; when conditions are bad, more compression is used, and audio quality is reduced. The aim of this is to keep the audio coming, even if it's of poor quality.

In order to stream audio, a computer must be set up by the resource owner to act as a server: its job will be to serve out audio on demand across the network. This needs to be a high-performance machine, and will require special audio streaming software. One of the commonest proprietary types of audio streaming on the web is currently RealAudio, from Real Networks Inc. For the user to hear RealAudio, they need a RealAudio plug-in for their browser. This plug-in communicates with the server software and downloads the sound bit by bit, playing it back as it goes.

To set up a streaming server will be fairly costly and will require specialist computing skills.

9.2.5. Usage considerations

The method of audio delivery you use will depend on what you think users will need to do with the sound.

If the purpose of the digital resource is to provide a source of optimum quality materials from which further copies are to be made, then the audio should be as close to the original as possible. It should probably not use compression, because even if the losses are seemingly imperceptible, some data is still lost; further processing at a later date may yield audibly different results than if the digitisation had been done without data compression. In this example, users will probably want to store the sound locally on their hard disk, in order to be able to make copies: so the sound should be downloadable.

If further copying or production work is not the aim, but the sounds are just there for people to listen to, then data compression (such as 'mp3') is appropriate: as discussed, this can greatly reduce download time with little or no perceptible loss of quality.

If you want users to be able to click an image or a link and hear sound immediately, they don't need a copy of the sound on their hard disk for later use, and sound quality is not of major importance, then streaming is most suitable. However, this is a resource-intensive method of delivering audio.

9.3. DISTRIBUTION AND ACCESS ISSUES

It may be that your negotiated copyright agreements require you to restrict access to the digitised audio. If the resource is distributed via CD-ROM only, this is easy as distribution can be controlled. However if the resource is delivered via the web, then it will be accessible to anyone. In fact this could dictate the way you deliver your resource.

However there are ways to implement access control on web sites. For instance, software can be used which prompts users for passwords. Users would need to apply to the resource owner, who can supply a password for that user. In this way, the number of users can be controlled. There are also ways to monitor web-resource usage, by counting the number of downloads of a particular soundfile for example. This could be used to determine what level of fee should be paid to rights holders in order to secure future use of that sound. Implementation of such systems will require specialist expertise in web technologies, though with such expertise they are perfectly feasible.

9.4. DESIGN CONSIDERATIONS

The decision about how to deliver audio content to users is essentially a technical one: whether to use streaming, compressed audio files, or uncompressed files is largely determined by your own technical resources and those of the potential user.

But it's important to consider visual impact too, even if the resource is mainly functional (such as a database or collection of research materials). A resource that is useful *and* interestingly put together has added value. Be aware of good design practice and bad design practice. For instance, there are web resources that present audio perfectly well technically speaking, but do so within the context of a fairly bland and/or poorly designed visual environment. There are some, however, which present audio in an innovative way, or in a visually exciting context, and there are plenty of software tools available to assist in the design and creation of web sites.

For examples of web sites that present audio materials in a variety of ways, refer to the PADS site at http://www.pads.ahds.ac.uk.

10. Preservation

There are two main aspects to ensuring the long-term preservation of digital audio data. The first concerns the life-span of digital storage media such as computer hard disk drives and removable media such as CDs. The second concerns sound file formats and obsolescence.

10.1. STORAGE MEDIA

Digital information held on computer hard disks and other digital media is not permanent. There are many factors which can result in the loss of data; these include mechanical failure (increasingly likely with age), electronic corruption (such as may be caused by errors in computer programmes, malicious viruses etc), and faults in magnetic or optical media (the material of the disk surface itself which stores the information). It is vital to take adequate steps to guard against such loss, both in the resource creation process and in the long term (i.e. beyond the life of the project, if the resource is to remain in place).

Digital audio media use 'error correction', which effectively smoothes over errors in the digital data, rendering them inaudible. Whilst this gives high audio quality, it does mean that the listener may be unaware of degradation in the medium until it becomes catastrophic and the medium becomes unplayable. The degradation of digital media used for archival purposes should be measured and monitored – see the IASA guidelines at http://www.llgc.org.uk/iasa/iasa0013.htm for more details.

Fortunately, backing up fairly small amounts of data is now relatively straightforward, using extra hard disks and removable media such as writable CDs. Specialist high-capacity long-term storage systems are also available, though they are costly.

The key to successful preservation is to have a strategy for backing up on a regular basis both during the creation process and once the resource is up and running. As any data is created, at least one backup copy should be made. This backup should be logged and stored safely. Once the creation process is complete, a long term strategy should take over. Such a strategy could be based on the following rules of thumb:

- If data in the resource changes often, backup often, and maybe make incremental backups rather than complete backups. How often will depend on the frequency and extent of the changes made.

- If data rarely or never changes, and the integrity of previous backups is reliable, then it makes sense to backup whenever changes are made or decide on some regular period for backing up.

Where a resource contains critical data it is advisable to seek specialist advice on preservation.

PADS will hold a preservation copy of your data too, but this should not be relied upon as delivering the data to users is your responsibility; in order to maintain service it is best to have a way of backing up and restoring your own data efficiently.

10.2. AUDIO FILE FORMATS

The other important aspect to consider is not just protection of the data itself, but also support for the format in which it is stored. This relates to the possible lifetime of sound file formats, and though this is not really currently an issue, it may be in future; it is important to stay informed about developments in audio file storage.

For instance, the 'wav' and 'aiff' formats are very common file formats today, and there is a huge amount of software that will deal with these files and play them back to users. They have been around for some years, and are likely to remain for the foreseeable future. But this may not always be the case. Though the standards will remain, there may be a time when they are superseded and other types of storage become more widespread; in this case some decision may need to be made about whether to convert files to more modern formats. Similarly, whilst the 'mp3' format is very common on the Internet just now, in future it may well be superseded by other higher performance methods for delivering audio.

A similar consideration has to be made regarding backup media, as storage capacities of media are likely to increase (as they have done dramatically in recent years), and the media themselves are likely to be displaced by newer high capacity systems. This is a continuous process in the computing field and it is important for resource creators and owners to stay in touch with new developments. Otherwise you may well be faced with having large quantities of data in essentially obsolete formats and media.

APPENDIX A – Glossary of terms

This is a glossary of common technical terms used in this guide.

AES/EBU	A digital audio signal standard, used for transmitting digital audio between devices. (developed jointly by the Audio Engineering Society and European Broadcasting Union)
AIFF	Common sound file format (Audio Interchange File Format)
Analogue	A continuously varying audio signal (in the form of an electrical voltage), as opposed to a digital signal.
analogue to digital converter	Electronic device that converts continuously varying signals to a stream of numbers.
attack transients	Short-lived high frequencies that occur at the onset of many types of sounds.
audio input	A socket or connector on a computer or piece of audio equipment which accepts a sound signal.
bits	'binary digits' – the ones and zeroes computers use to store numbers.
bit width	The number of bits, or binary digits, used to store each individual sound sample.
break-out box	A box that connects to a computer's audio hardware to give a more rugged set of connections than those found on the hardware itself.
Capture	Another term for recording
CD-ROM	Compact disk read-only-memory – CDs used to store data that cannot be overwritten. Writable CD-ROMs can be overwritten several times.
compression	Can mean either: data compression, where some existing data (such as a sound file) is reduced in size (such as in mp3 files); or audio compression, where the dynamic range of a sound signal is reduced.
Copyright	The right of a creator of a work to control its copying and dissemination.
cylinder	Phonograph cylinders – the earliest form of audio recording, where the cylinder surface is indented by a vibrating needle.
DAT	Digital Audio Tape – a common digital recording medium.

dbx	A type of noise reduction used by some analogue magnetic tape machines.
decibels	A ratio of the power of sound signals; a power ratio of 2:1 is equivalent to 3 decibels (3dB). The decibel can also be used to measure 'sound pressure level': the loudness of sounds.
decoding	Playing back a magnetic tape recording through a noise reduction system. The recording needs to have been encoded with noise reduction first.
digital to analogue	The process of converting a stream of numbers into a continuously varying signal.
digitisation	The process of converting analogue information into digital form.
distortion	Clicks, buzzing or other noise that results from a sound being recorded at too high a signal level.
Dolby	Dolby Laboratories: the company that developed Dolby Noise Reduction for magnetic audio media.
download	Copying a data file from the Internet onto a local computer.
encoding	Recording a sound onto magnetic tape through a noise reduction system, so as to reduce background hiss on playback.
EP	'Extended Play': the 7-inch 45 rpm vinyl record format introduced by RCA Victor in 1949.
extraction	The process of digitally transferring audio tracks from a CD direct to a computer's hard disk.
gramophone	The first lateral disk-based system for recording sound, developed by Emile Berliner in 1887.
hard disk	Device inside a computer used for long term mass storage of data.
Hertz	Cycles per second, the measure of frequency.
infringement	Illegal copying of material in which resides copyright.
input monitor	A setting in audio hardware allowing signals which are being recorded to be monitored at the same time.
Internet	The global computer network, allowing email to be sent anywhere in the world, and which hosts the 'world wide web'.
intranet	A local or private computer network.
line output	The connection on audio equipment from which an analogue sound signal comes.
LP	'Long Play': the 12-inch 33 rpm vinyl record format introduced by Columbia in 1948.
magnetic tape	Plastic tape coated with magnetic material used for sound recording.
megabyte	One million 'bytes', the measurement of computer data storage.

MIDI	A simple data transfer system that allows computers to communicate with synthesisers, music keyboards to communicate with computers etc.
mini-jacks	A type of small audio connector, common on low to mid range PC soundcards.
mix	A 'mix' of sounds; for instance, a film soundtrack is usually a mix of dialogue, background sounds and music.
mixing console	A device used for mixing and balancing audio signals, found in music studios.
modem	A device allowing a computer to connect to the Internet via telephone lines.
monitoring	Listening; usually the term is used when recording a sound.
motherboard	The main circuit board of a computer.
mp3	'Mp3', a type of compressed audio file. Actually a sound file which uses MPEG 1 Layer III encoding.
MPEG	Motion Picture Experts Group.
multitrack	Recording formats which allow several independent sound signals to be recorded onto the same medium simultaneously.
Noise reduction	Systems for reducing background hiss in magnetic tape recording.
Open reel	Common magnetic tape recording format, where tape is wound onto spools or reels.
operating system	The main programme of a computer that deals with its basic housekeeping tasks.
phonograph	The first sound recording device, using tin foil-coated, then wax, then shellac cylinders. Invented in 1877 by Thomas Edison.
processor	Either: a device for changing a sound in some way (as in 'effects processor'), or the calculating device at the heart of a computer (Central Processing Unit).
RAM	Random Access Memory: temporary storage space inside a computer.
RCA phono	A type of audio connector, common in hi-fi and some studio equipment.
records	Vinyl disks developed in the late 1940s for commercial dissemination of recorded music.
resolution	The accuracy at which sound is sampled or digitised.
sample resolution	The number of bits, or binary digits, used to store each individual sound sample.
sample width	The number of bits, or binary digits, used to store each individual sound sample.
sampling	The process of converting a sound signal into numbers or 'samples'.
sampling rate	The rate at which a sound is converted into numbers, in Hertz.

server	A computer on a network which serves out information to other computers.
signal-to-noise ratio	A measurement indicating the quality of audio electronic circuits: a high signal-to-noise ratio is good. Measured in decibels.
sound editor	A programme used for editing sound once digitised.
soundcard	The audio hardware inside a computer.
soundfile	A computer file containing sound data: the same as an audio file.
S/PDIF	The Sony/Philips Digital Interface, used for transmitting digital sound signals between equipment.
streaming	The process of sending and receiving audio or video over the Internet in 'real-time'.
WAV	Microsoft sound file format.
XLR	A type of audio connector, common in studios and professional audio equipment.

APPENDIX B – Bibliography

GENERAL ONLINE RESOURCES

American Memory – Historical Collections for the National Digital Library
http://memory.loc.gov/ammem/amhome.html (go to Collection Finder)

American Folklife Center – Omaha Indian Music
http://memory.loc.gov/ammem/omhhtml/omhhome.html

American Memory Sound Recording Collections
http://memory.loc.gov/ammem/audio.html

American Folklife Center – "Now What a Time": Blues, Gospel, and the Fort Valley Music
Festivals, 1938–1943
http://memory.loc.gov/ammem/ftvhtml/ftvhome.html

BBC Digital Arts
http://www.bbc.co.uk/arts/digital/index.shtml

bits and pieces: a sonic installation for the web
http://www.fictive.org/~peter/bits/index.html

Ceolas – Celtic Music on the Internet
http://ceolas.org/ceolas.html

Digital Music Archives
http://www.digital-music-archives.com/

Digitisation – An Introduction
http://www.bufvc.ac.uk/maas/technology/index.html

IASA Technical Committee Standards
The Safeguarding of the Audio Heritage: Ethics, Principles and Preservation Strategy
http://www.llgc.org.uk/iasa/iasa0013.htm

peoplesound
http://www.peoplesound.com

Sound Practice: conference on sound, culture and environments
http://www.soundpractice.org.uk

Symphony for Cornwell
http://www.symphony.cornwall.dmu.ac.uk/

Sonic Arts Network
http://www.sonicartsnetwork.org/ (go to 'sounds')

UBUWEB: Visual, Concrete and Sound Poetry
http://www.ubu.com

UK Patent Office
http://www.patent.gov.uk/copy/

University of Iowa Musical Instrument Samples page
http://theremin.music.uiowa.edu/~web/sound/

METADATA RESOURCES
GENERAL CATALOGUING AND METADATA STANDARDS/FRAMEWORKS

Anglo-American Cataloguing Rules, second edition, 1998 revision

Dublin Core Metadata Initiative
http://dublincore.org

Getty Institute Metadata Resources
http://www.getty.edu/research/institute/standards/intrometadata/

Library of Congress Metadata Resources
http://www.loc.gov/standards/metadata.html

OCLC Cataloging Internet Resources
http://www.oclc.org/oclc/man/9256cat/toc.htm

Resource Description Framework (RDF)
http://www.w3.org/RDF/

UKOLN Interoperability
http://www.ukoln.ac.uk/metadata/interoperability/

CLASSIFICATION SCHEMES

Dewey Decimal Classification
http://www.oclc.org/dewey/index.htm

Library of Congress Classification Outline
http://lcweb.loc.gov/catdir/cpso/lcco/lcco.html

Universal Decimal Classification Consortium
http://www.udcc.org/

AUDIO-VISUAL CATALOGUING AND METADATA

HARMONICA II Accompanying Action on Music Information in Libraries
http://www.svb.nl/project/harmonica/Deliverables/D141.htm

International Association of Audio-Visual Archives
http://www.llgc.org.uk/iasa/index.htm

The IASA cataloguing rules
http://www.llgc.org.uk/iasa/icat/index.htm

International Association of Music Libraries, Archives and Documentation Centres
http://www.cilea.it/music/iaml/iamlhome.htm

Music Cataloguing Guidelines from the American Music Library Association
http://www.lib.duke.edu/music/sheetmusic/title.html

AUTHORITY SOURCES FOR PROPER NAMES

New Grove Dictionary of Music and Musicians Online
http://www.grovemusic.com/

The Internet movie database
http://www.imdb.com/

ONLINE JOURNALS

Ariadne Online Journal
http://www.ariadne.ac.uk/

D-Lib Forum and Magazine
http://www.dlib.org/